A Classic in Plywood

How to Build the Gloucester Light Dory

Harold "Dynamite" Payson

Photographs by Jeff Julian

Plans by Philip C. Bolger

WoodenBoat Books

Published by WoodenBoat Publications, Inc.
Naskeag Road
Brooklin, Maine 04616

Second printing 1986
Third printing 1988

Library of Congress Cataloging-in-Publication Data

Payson, Harold H.
  How to build the Gloucester light dory.

  Bibliography: p.
  1. Dories (Boats)—Design and construction—Handbooks, manuals,
etc. I. Title.
VM351.P36 1986   623.8′29   86-15960
ISBN 0-937822-04-3 (pbk.)

Foreword

Dynamite Payson, a definition—*A short, agreeable man, residing in a mostly bucolic setting near the mouth of the 'Keag River where it empties into Maine's Penobscot Bay. Lobsterman, boatbuilder, sometimes smelt fisherman; slow-talker, fast-acter, characterized by expressiveness of the highest order ("Bending that plank was tougher than chewing boiled owls"). Honest, straightforward, one of a dying breed of competent mechanics in the old-fashioned sense of the word.*

Like thousands of boat lovers, I knew Dynamite Payson long before I met him, having answered one of his classified advertisements in a boating magazine. In the return mail came a packet of information on Downeast Dories, spiced with an aura of boatiness that promised the realization of my dreams for the perfect rowing boat—the Gloucester Gull, since evolved into the Gloucester Light Dory. Dynamite's personality came through in the literature, and I knew right then that I must meet this man.

That was more than 10 years ago, and the intervening time has found me amused, amazed, and appreciative of the visits I have made to the boatshop and home of Dynamite Payson.

Dynamite, like many Mainers, is a curious blend of contradictions. A traditionalist, he builds most of his boats in plywood. Cautiously conservative, he builds prototypes of some of Phil Bolger's most avant-garde designs. An introvert, he is a consummate conversationalist. A stay-at-homer, he has incredible curiosity about the outside world. A perfectionist, he is artful at compromise.

Dynamite's most endearing strength is his willingness to share his knowledge and skill, a trait that is rare among boatbuilders who much prefer to take their secrets to the grave on the assumption that techniques made public are the seeds of undesirable competition. If you ask, he'll explain—in person, in print, even on videotape if you should so desire—yet every amateur instructed in boatbuilding is a potential customer lost, because Dynamite's first order of business (at least since he gave up lobster fishing a few years ago) is building boats for sale.

Knowing Dynamite, it came as no surprise that when we asked him to describe the building of that most elegant of light rowing dories, he agreed with alacrity. His three-part series, "A Classic in Plywood" which appeared in WoodenBoat Nos. 41-43, is gathered together in this short dissertation for those who can appreciate that the best is simplicity itself.

—Peter H. Spectre

GLOUCESTER LIGHT DORY

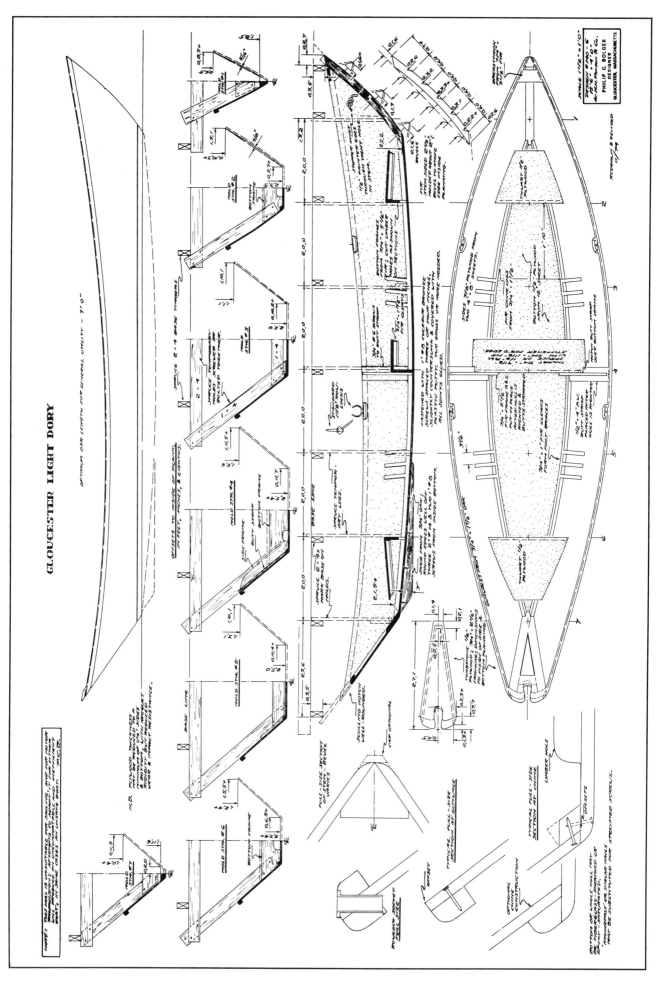

OPTIMUM OAR LENGTH FOR GENERAL UTILITY - 7'0"

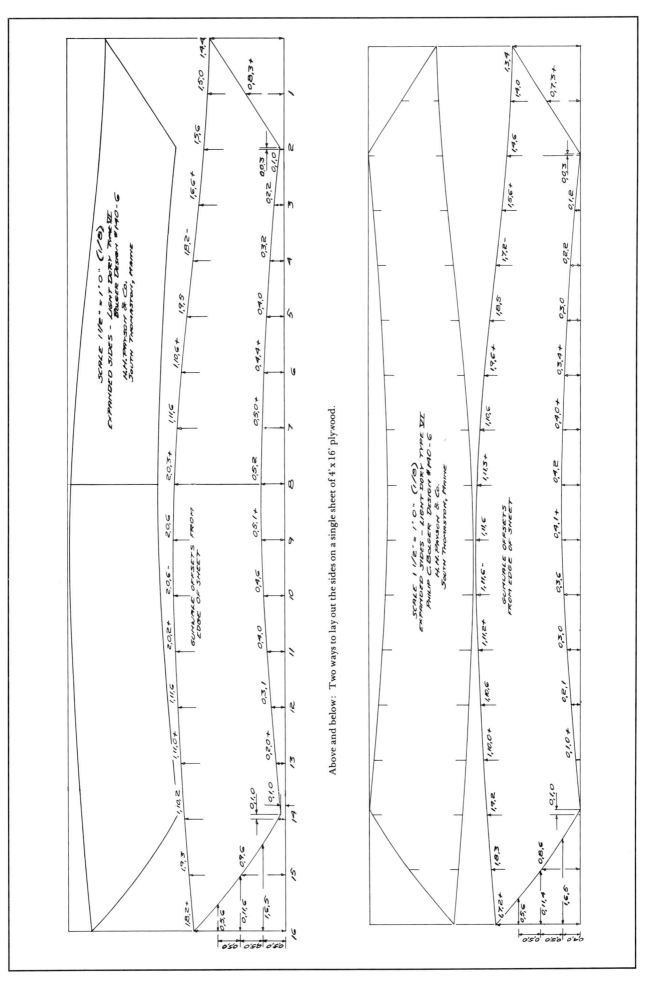

Above and below: Two ways to lay out the sides on a single sheet of 4' x 16' plywood.

5

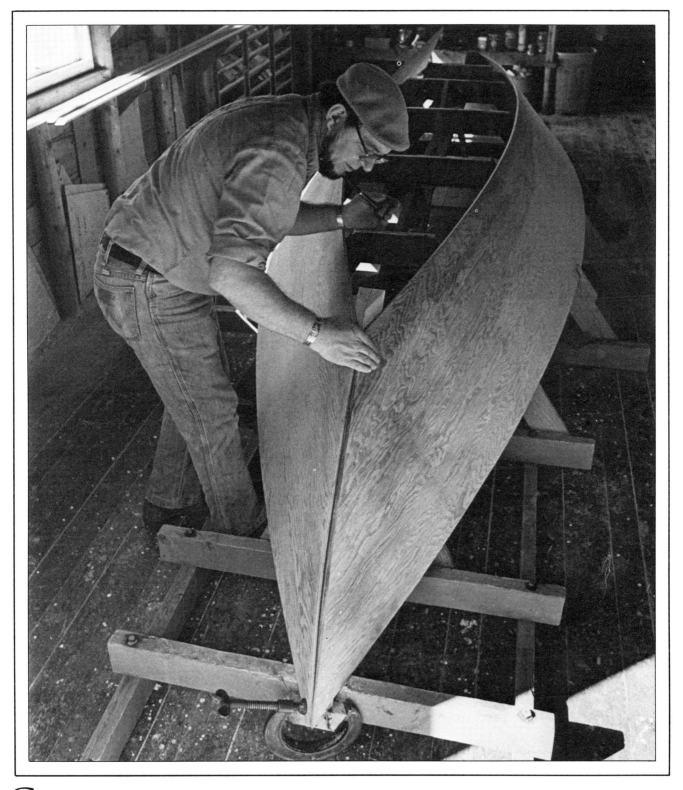

Call it what you will—Gloucester Light Dory, Gloucester Gull, Type VI—whatever. The fast, light rowing dory probably has names you and I can't pronounce, or even spell, because this craft has graced the waters of countries all over the world, including Russia.

Its history began unmomentously back in the 1950s when Philip C. Bolger, N.A., of Gloucester, Massachusetts, pulled out of retirement an

old design of his called the Golden River—a planked-up lapstrake round-sided dory. It was a good deal lower and slimmer than the usual working dory and consequently much easier to row. It was decidedly *not* easier to build. In fact, its construction was so finicky and laborious that you can count the roster of completed Golden Rivers on the fingers of one hand, even if you are a careless sawmill worker.

"I decided to revamp it for sheet

plywood construction," Phil Bolger says now, "and in a moment of inspiration very much improved the looks of the sheerline."

Bolger built one that winter. He makes no claim to competence as a boat carpenter: "A kind friend said to me, 'If you stand back about 50', that boat looks real good.'"

His original aim was to provide an easily rowed tender for his leeboard sharpie POINTER, which he launched

Drawings by Frank O'Brien

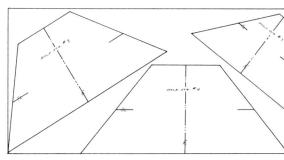

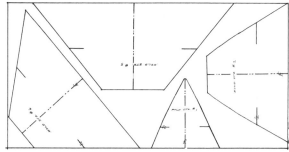

Using offsets provided in the construction plan, the station molds are laid out on sheet plywood. With care and planning, all seven molds can be cut from two sheets of 1/2" or 3/4" plywood.

in the summer of 1960. The sharpie had no deck room to stow a dinghy, and he needed a tender that could survive rough water when he had to row some distance to and from an offshore anchorage. Let Phil tell it.

"I gave the dory a quick trial, hurriedly added a skeg to make her tow straight and took off for a month's cruise around Cape Cod and adjacent islands. The intent was to show off the sharpie, but wherever I went, nobody looked at her. Their eyes were all trained astern of her, at the dory on the end of the painter. She got so many compliments I began to think I had a commercial product, so when I got home I redesigned it for production building.

"Art Rand's boat shop built upwards of 50, then Art got into a financial bind that put him out of business. For vanity's sake I wanted the design to stay in circulation, so I redrew the plans once again and presented that version to Captain Jim Orrell, the Texas Dory man.

"He called it the Gloucester Gull and circulated it nobly; he must have sent out thousands of plans. Then he got angry because I wouldn't draw up a sailing rig and a motor well for it, and in turn I lost my temper because he went ahead and found somebody else to do both over my objections. I felt that these should have been

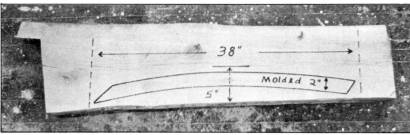

On the best part of an oak plank, the stem pattern is traced.

After rough-cutting the oak to a manageable size, the stem is cut to shape on the bandsaw.

Clamped in the vise, the stem is planed smooth. A spokeshave works well for the inside curve.

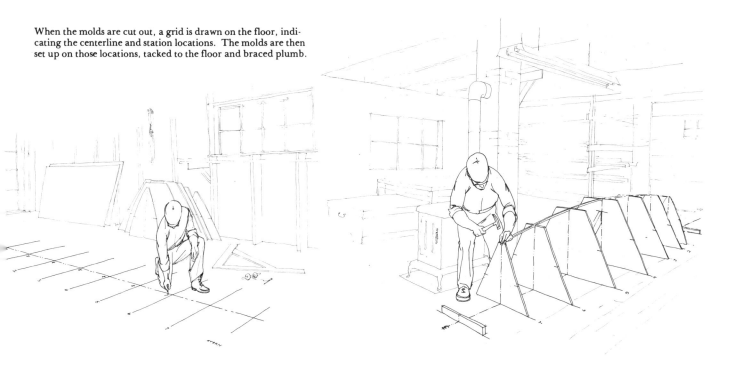

When the molds are cut out, a grid is drawn on the floor, indicating the centerline and station locations. The molds are then set up on those locations, tacked to the floor and braced plumb.

respected, because I knew that either one of these modifications meant not only an inefficient boat but also a dangerous one.

"The absolute final version, so far as I'm concerned, is the Type VI. This one was drawn to Harold Payson's order. He both builds them and sells the plans, which is the way it should be, ideally. I think it must have been one of his boats in which the hero of 'Swashbuckler' pursued the heroine of that otherwise disappointing movie."

Enter me—Harold H. (Dynamite) Payson.

The year 1967 found me building a variety of skiff types as a way of treading water until I could see what course to take in the boatbuilding game. I was in no hurry to jump at just anything, because I was making my living as a lobster fisherman. Building boats meant simply doing what I enjoyed most, whether it made financial sense or not.

For quite some years before that, I had been building round-bottom carvel-planked boats, and doing very well at it. Then came fiberglass. Came? It came like an avalanche. For a while you could even buy a fiberglass boat at your friendly local service station, a cloned copy—maybe a day's work in glass—of what I was spending a month turning out by

smoothing progresses, use the trisquare ertain that the fore and aft faces are to the sides.

When the smoothing is complete, use the trisquare to strike centerlines on the fore and aft faces of the stem.

The stem bevel of 30 degrees is rough-cut on the bandsaw, leaving enough wood to smooth up to the lines by hand.

hand. You could even float a loan to buy the boat, if you didn't have the cash.

It didn't take a magnifying glass to read the handwriting on the wall: *make it out of glass, sell it quickly, and forget it.* Which I did not want to do. I could not turn my back on cedar shavings, clouds of steam softening up frames, and all the other sights, sounds, and smells that said boat to me. Hence the one-man skiff factory—to keep my eye and hand in practice.

One day Eugene Swan, owner of Pine Island Boy's Camp in the Belgrade Lakes region of Maine, walked into my shop and said: "Dynamite, how about building a dory for the boys?"

"Nope. I'm not interested."

Likely my reply came from an instant flashback to boyhood days when I was rowing a Banks dory around a string of lobster pots and getting blown all over the ocean by winds that my 128 pounds, boots and all, couldn't begin to manage. There was another reason for my reply. I had seen too many plans, boats too, for that matter, which were based on the idea that a very small dory was just the thing for kids who wanted to learn how to row. But teaching them to drown was their most likely function.

I considered the matter closed and thought Eugene did, too. But the next time he showed up, a few months later, he unfolded a set of plans, spread them on my workbench and said, "Look at this."

I took a quick look, then a much longer one. I was looking at the Gloucester Gull.

"How many do you want?" I asked him after a while. He wanted three.

Since that day I have built more than a hundred, and have helped launch God knows how many hundreds more by selling plans.

It wasn't just the lovely lines that made me want to build to Bolger's design. It was also a matter of building style. The hull lends itself to building upside down on a jig, just the way I had been doing with the skiffs— put the stem and stern in place, fasten the sides to them, put the chines in and the bottom on, then pull the hull off, and there you are, all done so far as the basic hull shape is concerned.

That part can be done in a day, once you have made patterns for everything, as I have. Add 40 hours to do all the woodwork, after you have assembled the transom, cut the stem to shape, and readied chines and gunwales to go in—all part of the preassembly, the way I do it. Total time, including fiberglassing the bottom, painting the hull, and giving it time to dry, is a little under two weeks.

That's my schedule, as a professional builder. Starting from scratch as you will be doing, by the time you build the jig, take your side patterns off that, and make one-off versions of all the parts I prefabricate and stockpile in advance, you can bet on a month between the day you gather your materials and the day you lug your dory out of the shop.

I'm not suggesting that you make a race against time out of building this boat. There's no need to hurry it. But people who set out to build a boat do prefer to have a pretty good idea when launching day is going to dawn, since they also have other work to perform and schedules to meet. But, whatever percentage of your time you can devote to boatbuilding, one thing is sure: One hour of planning is worth two of work. So begin by brooding over the scaled building plans. With these sheets before you, and an architect's scale in hand, settle yourself comfortably away from all distractions and *build the boat in your head.* I guarantee that this approach will take a comfortable slice off your actual building time, because it will minimize the type of mistakes that mean doing things twice.

The scale rule is one of your most valuable tools. On the plans, just above the box with the designer's name, is the notation *Scale: $1^1/2'' = 1'0''$.* So use that side of your triangular architect's rule to find any measurement that is not immediately clear to you. The rule can also serve as a key to boat terminology that may be unfamiliar to you. For example, you're told that the stem is sided $2^1/2''$ and molded about $2''$. Your scale rule shows the width athwartships at the

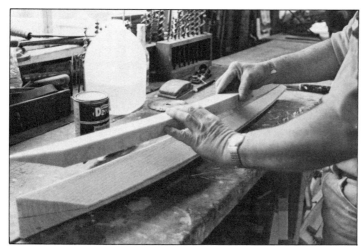

When both sides have been beveled, the waste is saved intact, to be temporarily fastened back in place.

A few small nails will suffice to tack each waste piece back to the stem.

top is 2¹/₂" and the fore-and-aft profile of the stem is approximately 2"—so now you know what sided and molded mean.

A technicality peculiar to marine construction plans is the system of indicating measurements. They are always expressed in three numerals, such as 2-4-5. These are respectively feet, inches, and eighths of inches, so those numbers represent 2', 4", and 5/8". If there is a plus following the last digit, add 1/16". Tables of offsets are always expressed this way.

I have no way of knowing just how much an individual reader already knows about boatbuilding. The reason I am writing this is to put something in the hands of prospective builders that will answer any question they may have. I have carried on hour-long telephone conversations with purchasers of these dory plans. Some of these dialogues reveal abysmal ignorance of what are to me, as a professional, such self-evident concepts that I need never consciously think of them; they are in the air I breathe. I have never been irked by such inquiries; I'm pleased that the caller is seriously involved enough to get in touch with me.

What does bother me is the realization that somewhere out there in would-be-boatbuilder-land there must be dozens, maybe hundreds of people who have the same questions but don't track me down for answers. In my mind's eye I see their sets of perfectly

good plans curling and crackling in the fireplace, or used to wrap up garbage. I am writing for these potential builders, as well as those with better, but varying, degrees of understanding of building procedure.

So, for some of my readers I will be guilty of overkill. If you are among them, bear with me and profit from what you can.

I might suggest that if you are timid about starting right in to build your first boat, make a scale model instead. It costs almost nothing and is a great way to learn how to use the scale rule.

The Setting Up Exercise

The most frequently, and most plaintively, asked question I run into is: *How do I begin?*

You begin with the baseline, which is shown in the profile view of the plans, and again on mold station No. 5, as a straight line directly over and along the top of 2x4 longitudinals that serve as a support for the molds at each of their stations. The molds are erected so they are plumb and square to the baseline. Think of the baseline as the imaginary spine of the boat—the axis of its universe, if you will.

Step one in applying this concept is setting up—the construction of a jig that will support the molds around which you will bend the sides, to the stem at the bow and the transom at the stern. There are two ways of

approaching this stage. The setup shown in the plans is called the *ladder frame* method, and if you use it you will construct a permanent jig based on the aforementioned longitudinal 2x4s—a structure that will include the molds.

I don't advise the ladder frame method, even though it was my choice, because I am a production boatbuilder. My structure has survived the production of more than 100 hulls and 14 winters of outside storage at the time of writing. Unless you plan to build quite a few boats, or lend your jig to friends to use in building theirs, forget it.

If you do plan to build such a jig, here is what you will need for materials:

2 2x4s, 16' long, for longitudinal supports

9 2x4s, 12' long, for cross members

80 lineal feet of rough-sawn 1x4" spruce, pine, fir, or what-have-you for mold-station framing and bracing off the molds (planed boards are OK, but not as strong)

18 1/4" or 5/16" carriage bolts with nuts and washers to bolt the cross members to the longitudinals

1 gross—1¹/₂" No. 10 galvanized screws to fasten the mold frame corners (three for each joint, 12 per mold)

All this will cost you about $70, right now, and who knows how much a year from now. It will also cost you many hours of patient, meticulous

With one waste piece tacked on, the stem can be clamped in the vise to be planed to the lines.

As the smoothing nears completion, check the bevel with the side of the plane to insure that the plywood will lie properly against the stem.

When the bevels are properly finished, a wood rasp is used to remove the sharp corners on the aft face.

work cutting and aligning all those pieces, and boring for and driving the bolts.

Instead, I recommend a method that will cost you about $20. This way, you build your molds from 1/2" or 3/4" plywood, particleboard, or any other material that is both stiff and cheap. You can cut all seven molds from two 4x8' sheets, marked and cut full size from the material, with no corners to align and no elements to screw together.

If you have a level wooden floor, let that be your baseline and just plunk the molds down at the proper intervals, making sure they're centered on the centerline. (The centerline is just the baseline as viewed from above — an imaginary line running right down the middle of your theoretical boat.) Snap a chalk line to establish your centerline — or adopt a straight floor seam for it, if there is one.

If your floor is not level, set up a couple of longitudinals and shore them up until they are level, then erect your molds on them.

Remember one thing while you're marking off the locations for the molds: beginning with mold No. 3 and proceeding forward, they are placed *aft* of the station marks; the after molds working toward the stern are set *forward* of the station marks. This eliminates the need to bevel the molds to follow the curve of the hull. Instead, you can bend your sides right to the edge they fall on. So when you saw out your molds, leave them square. Place an X exactly where each mold is to go, so you won't hear yourself saying, a little later, *My God — I've got one on the wrong side of the mark.*

If you're using the ladder-frame method and making your molds out of 1x4 stock, make a full-size drawing and lay your framing right on the drawing. Cut, fit, and assemble the molds right there.

If, as I strongly recommend, you are instead cutting your molds from plywood sheets, proceed as follows:

Start with mold No. 4. Flip your plywood sheet onto a couple of sawhorses. The bottom edge of the sheet represents the athwartships plane of the baseline — you can use the whole 8' edge as your baseline. Checking your plans with your scale rule, you find that the distance from the center of mold No. 4 to its outside edge at the baseline is 2'11" — that is its half-breadth. Give yourself a little leeway, so measure in from the 4' edge of the sheet an even 3' and erect your perpendicular from that point. Don't bother to use a square — your plywood sheet is cut absolutely square, so just measure in 3' from the end along the 8' edge opposite your baseline edge and connect the two points. There is your centerline, a vertical that is 3' in from one 4' edge of the sheet, so mark it "Centerline."

Now you want to establish the height of that mold from the baseline, and its width at that point — in other words, the location and the width of the inside of the bottom of your boat. The figure for the height is 2-5-4 plus. So measure along the centerline, up from the baseline, 2'5" and 1/2" plus 1/16" — 2'5^9/^{16}".

Half the width of the bottom is 0-11-7, so you measure horizontally from the centerline, at the height you've just located, 11^7/^{8}" in both directions, and you connect these points. You can use a square, but I trust measurements from the edge of a plywood sheet more, because you can more accurately join marks a long distance apart. Besides, a framing square used on plywood can get knocked askew by glue buildup without your noticing it; an out-of-whack line is the result.

Next, establish the height of the sheer at mold No. 4, marking it along the centerline 1-2-6 above the baseline. That is 1'2^3/^{4}", right? And there, measuring out horizontally from the centerline, put a mark at 1-11-5 plus on each side. That's 1'11^{11}/^{16}" each way for a total of 2'2^3/^{8}" for the width of the sheer.

Now take a straightedge and connect the ends of the bottom and the

Set the stem in place on the jig, being sure that it is both centered, plumb and at the right height. Nail it temporarily in place.

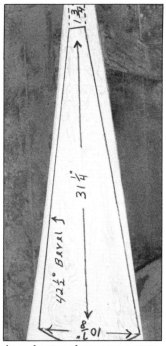

As on the stem, the transom pattern is traced out — this time on a piece of plywood. (The dimensions and bevels are marked here for purposes of clarity.)

Begin by cutting the transom bevels at 42½ deg on the bandsaw. Then, with the saw set square the remaining cuts are made.

sheer widths, and you have drawn the flare of the sides at mold No. 4.

That's how the molds are drawn; all you do now is repeat the process for the other molds. Molds No. 1 and 2 require a slight curvature, which you must add on—5/16" for No. 1 and 3/8" for No. 2.

If you're using the 1x4 framing of the ladder-frame jig method, keep your top assembly screws inboard along the chines so they won't be in the way when you cut the corners off the jig to let the chines in. If you're using plywood molds, no problem, because no screws are used. The corners will be cut later after you've laid a batten along the molds to take off the shapes of the boat's sides, unless you use my side patterns. But, first, we have to make the stem and the tombstone transom, both of which will be shaped, beveled, and put in place on the jig before we take off the shape of the expanded sides.

Begin at Both Ends

I'm no alcoholic, not yet, anyway, but that part of the Alcoholic's Prayer which speaks of things that can be changed and things that cannot, and the need for wisdom to know the difference, strikes me as very relevant to the frustrated tyro who, for the very first time, comes up against a set of naval architect's plans—everything nice and neat, all perfectly fitted to a hair's breadth—and tries to duplicate that perfection in wood.

I know of nothing that will make you a believer any quicker than working with a piece of wood, which can be as contrary as hell, and completely unforgiving when it comes to mistakes. To make his life bearable, the skilled boat carpenter draws on past experience to judge just where precise fitting is needed, and where it is not—and, if he makes mistakes, to recognize what he can change and what he can't.

Such judgment is something no one can give you, because the building of every boat varies from those before and those after, but by building a variety of boats over a period of time, your educated eye will be able to pick up at a glance those joints that demand such perfection, and you will be able to tell your educated hands just how much leeway they have in achieving that perfection the easiest way.

Until that time, the most helpful rule to follow is to, whenever possible, *leave it long, and cut it off later.*

I've seen much boat construction needlessly screwed up because a cut was made before it was necessary and before all the facts were in—say a bevel needlessly cut beforehand, or frames needlessly cut to fit in advance and whose ends didn't quite make it when the bend was put in. This dory is full of pitfalls like that, so, please let's have no rushes to judgment.

To this day, I don't know the exact technique Phil Bolger had in mind for the building of this boat. Do you put the chines in first, and fit the sides to them? You could (but only in theory). Or do you put the sides in place first, and fit the chines inside them? The latter method is much easier, and past experience tells me to do it that way: big pieces first, stem and transom in place, nail the sides on, then put the chines in, fasten the bottom on, and you have a boat. That's my way, and it works; let's do it.

Assuming the jig is built and the molds are set in place—properly aligned and firmly braced against movement—we will start with the stem.

Shaping the Stem

Find a piece of oak, 3'x5"x2½". That's about 2" longer than the stem layout calls for, but there's your margin of safety. If you can, utilize the grain to advantage when you lay the stem out—if there's a grain curving with or close to the stem profile, go with it.

Make a paper or wood pattern from the diagram on the plan by striking a succession of straight, parallel lines at the intervals shown, with each

The outboard edges of the transom frames are also cut at a 42½ degree bevel, but the straight cut is more easily made on a table saw.

The transom frame stock is cut long enough to provide two frames with some extra, and the first one is aligned and clamped so that the bevels match up flush.

line squared off at the fore-and-aft faces of the stem. Drive in brads—1" No. 18 wire or something of the sort—at the squared ends. Strike fair curves to the extreme end of the lower part of the stem. Leave the excess to be sawn off later. Lay this pattern on the oak stock you've chosen, and carefully trace both curves. Use your bandsaw to cut both sides square to the profile shape.

Using a combination square, immediately mark the centerline on both the forward and the after faces. This is a must, because the after centerline must match the centerline of mold No. 1, and the forward centerline will be used for working the stem bevel down to the leading, or cutwater, edge.

Bevel the stem as shown in the plans: $1^3/4$" at the head, $1^7/8$" at the midpoint, and back to $1^3/4$" at the foot. Thirteen years have passed since I laid out the first Gloucester Gull stem, and I can't remember whether the bevels were right then or not. When you lay out what the designer shows, full size on paper, the bevels appear to be a bit on the short side—that is, there is less bevel than needed, which is good, as that leaves extra wood that can be taken off; far better than over beveling, which would make the sides lie poorly.

Anyway, it's safe to cut the bevel as shown. Then put the stem in place on the jig and nail it to station 1 and the cross member. Spring a thin, limber batten along the molds so it touches at least three molds and protrudes past the face of the stem. The batten shows how the plywood sides will lie on the boat, so you can see how much wood, if any, will have to be taken off the molds to achieve a fair curve.

I fit the chines after the sides are on and butt the chines against the stem. This practice can leave a gap between the skin of the boat and the bottom of the stem (though the design doesn't show it). In addition, the extra protuberance of the stem leaves a crack for paint runs and crud-catching. To avoid these gaps, I make my stem sided $2^5/8$" instead of $2^1/2$", and I extend the bevel out to within 1/8" or less from the after edge of the stem. The 2" molded dimension stays the same.

Beveling is simple. Just set your combination square to mark a line parallel to the after side of the stem, 1/8" in from the edge, then set your bandsaw at 30 degrees. Start the cut from the top of the stem, keeping the face against the table, and saw to that 1/8" line, cutting a wedge-shaped piece from both sides. Keep these scrap pieces, and tack one of them right back on to give you bearing for clamping the stem in the vise.

That 30-degree setting spares the centerline by a wide margin, which is what you want. If you were to cut right on the line, thus obliterating it, you wouldn't have any guide for working the stem down to its leading edge. Do your final beveling at the vise; with the bulk of the wood already removed by the bandsaw, it will take only a few minutes to work the bevel down to the centerline.

Mark the locations of the sheer and chine on the stem, which is now ready for installation. Place a cleat on the jig for the top of the stem to bear on, and bevel its ends so you can hook clamps over the cleat to haul the sides in against the stem later on.

Making the Tombstone Transom

The view of the transom on the drawing, with all its measurements and

The second transom frame is positioned so the bevels match, and a long mitre line is marked and cut where the two converge at the bottom of the transom.

When the joint and the bevels are matched and clamped, the filler for the sculling notch is marked and cut to fit in place on the transom. Leaving the excess stock, glue and fasten the pieces in place.

Setting the transom in place on the jig is again a matter of getting it centered, plumb, and at the proper height. Nail it in place.

bevels, is the same view you will see when it's all nicely fitted in the boat. When you look at the drawing for the first time, bearing in mind that you have to cut a pair of sides to make those perfect joints, you will want to hit the bottle. You probably won't but you will quickly understand why at least part of the builder's time is best spent figuring out the easiest way to build what the designer has drawn, however complicated it may seem. No criticism of the designer is intended; he's shown everything that needs to be shown. It's up to the builder to interpret the evidence and reproduce the design.

Forget the top of the transom and the bottom bevel for now. The most important project at the moment is to shape the tombstone and bevel to specifications where the sheer and chine lines fall.

Note on the plan that 2-7-1 is the total length measured from the extreme bottom bevel of the transom framing to the transverse curve of the top. Project the outer dotted lines, which represent the inner face of the plywood transom, in both directions. At the top of the transom this gives you a width of 11''; at the bottom, 1³/₄''.

On a piece of 1/2'' plywood 2'8''x 11'', mark a vertical centerline, then measure off 2-7-1 from the bottom edge, leaving the scant inch of excess on the top.

Project half of the 11'' and 1³/₄'' measurements on each side of the centerline, top and bottom, and connect these points to establish the side flare of the transom.

From the 2-7-1 mark at the top, measure 0-1-3 plus and 0-3-7 to find the inner and outer marks for the sheer. Crown this edge, if you like, but leave the excess plywood for trimming later.

The rest is easy. Cut the plywood transom side bevels with a 42¹/² degree setting, and cut two pieces of 3/4x2¹/²x42'' oak framing to the same bevel. Match the bevels of the transom and the frames together, letting the ends of the framing extend beyond the bottom of the transom by an inch or so to be trimmed later. Glue and fasten the transom parts together, driving 1¹/₈'' Anchorfast-type nails from the plywood into the oak. Be careful to locate the nails so they will not be in the way when the top is trimmed to shape later. Keep them back from the ends of the bot-

tom frame pieces as well, because you will be trimming there also.

The sculling notch insert is best made from cedar, pine, spruce, or fir. These woods are better than oak for this purpose, because they are less susceptible to splitting or warping and have better gluing qualities. Draw in the approximate scull notch outline, and keep nails clear of it when you glue and fasten the notch insert in place.

Use your scale rule when determining the placement of both the stem and the transom in your building setup. For the transom, the distance from the baseline to the bottom of the transom frame bevel is 2-1-5 plus. With the height of the transom on the jig thus established, match its centerline with that of the jig and fasten it with a couple of 5d galvanized nails through the oak framing.

The corresponding measurement for the stem is 2-2-2. The designer hasn't made these dimensions specifically clear in either case, but you have your scale rule, and this is one of the reasons I emphasize its frequent use.

With molds, transom, and stem in place, your setup is complete. Time for a moment of celebration. The

a 2' x 16' sheet of plywood, side is cut to shape.

Bent around the molds and clamped in place, the unusual shape of the side suddenly makes sense. The bevel planed into the clamping face of the stem allows the upper clamp to be placed at the corner of the stem without slipping off under pressure.

The side is glued to the stem and fastened with 1¹/₈'' Anchorfast nails into prebored holes. Remember to set the heads below flush with a nail set.

next step will be shaping and installing the sides, and we'll continue with that in the next section.

Shaping and Installing the Sides

A couple of pages back, I mentioned receiving phone calls from puzzled dory builders. One call that puzzled me was from a man who was having chine troubles. I couldn't get a handle on his problem for the better part of a half hour. When I was patiently describing, for perhaps the third time, the step-by-step process of installing the chines, and getting nowhere, I suddenly realized that he did not yet have the sides in place. What he was trying to do was hang his chines in mid-air, so to speak—a particularly difficult exercise, considering he had to deal with a two-way bend and a 10-degree twist in an unyielding 12' length of dry oak anchored in the stem at one end and the transom at the other.

Using building practices current some years ago, this would have been perfectly feasible, and was in fact standard practice if your molds were designed to remain an integral part of the finished hull. With the latter technique, you can install your chines and inwales, fastening them firmly on each mold as well as the stem and the tran-

som, before you lay the sides against them.

Not so with this dory. First you must make a pattern for the two side pieces, mount them in place, and then slip the chines in against them.

You can use my side pattern if you wish, or take off your own from your jig or building setup. This method is simple and infallibly accurate, and you can use it on a number of the hulls I sell plans for, such as the small daysailer called the Thomaston Galley or the speedy utility power dory known as the Sea Hawk.

Begin by cutting two light, straight battens of 1x3/8" stock—a 12-footer for the chine and a 16-footer for the sheer. Knot-free pine is good for battens, but anything that will bend in a fair curve is OK.

Tack the 12' batten along the chine line, fastening it at the stem, the corner of each mold, and the transom. Similarly, fasten the 16' piece at each sheer mark on those locations. Now take a 3x16' piece of building paper—the cheap orange kind—and lay it right over the battens, stretching it a little to avoid wrinkles and edge-set. Staple it in place, and trace all around the battens, along the face of the stem, and down the transom. Remove the paper and cut out the traced pattern with extreme care.

At this point I'm going to assume

you are using a single 4x16' sheet of 3/8" marine plywood for your sides, rather than butting two 8' pieces together. I'll get back to the butting approach in a minute.

Cut that 16' sheet lengthwise right down the middle so you have two 2x16' pieces. Place your pattern on one of the halves, putting a substantial weight on one end while you tug to remove any small wrinkles. When the pattern is absolutely smooth, weight the second end too. Trace the pattern, and you're ready to cut one side.

The portable circular saw is the tool to use, although a saber saw will do in a pinch. Incidentally, the portable circular saw will come in handy for so many cuts on this boat that you'd do well to buy or borrow one for the duration of the project.

Adjust the blade so it will just barely cut through the wood. This setting gives good steering control plus safety; if you set the blade for a deeper cut, you will lose something on both counts. As you cut, don't saw to the line; rather, leave about 1/4" all around the traced line.

Next put the sawn panel on the set-up, with the battens still in place, and check the accuracy of your tracing and sawing. Make sure the ends of the panel are twisted in to lie flat against the stem and the transom, and also

The inside chine used by the autho[r] laid out by means of his 6' folding [rule] the corner of which butts up again[st] the stem.

After marking out the thickness of transom and frame on the side, the glue is spread and the side fastened in place.

The other side is fastened in the same way, and guided into place by leveling with the first side.

against every mold. You'll need clamps for this, of course.

Trace around the battens for a final fit, still leaving 1/2" or so overhang at the transom for later trimming. While you're at it, double check the molds to make certain that none of them is higher than it should be; if so, it will interfere with the bottom planking. When you are satisfied that all's well, make four wooden thumb cleats and fasten them at the sheer marks on molds 3 and 5. They will be a great aid in putting the panels back exactly in place, especially if you are working alone.

Remove the side panel, make a duplicate, and remove the battens from the setup; you're through with them.

At this point, cut the corners out of each mold to allow them to receive the chine. *You must* do this now, *before* you fasten the sides permanently in place.

You will be using glue and 1¹/₈" Anchorfast nails to fasten the sides. If the oak of your stem and the transom frame has some moisture in it, prebore for the nails with a 5/64" drill; if it's bone dry, go to a 3/32" drill.

Now for the glue. Mix up any marine glue of your choice. I use Weldwood dry powder mixed with water, which is plenty strong enough when properly concocted. For mixing containers, I use half-pint milk cartons

with the tops sliced off; a 1/2" depth of powder in one of these will make up sufficient quantity to glue both side panels to the stem and the transom. Mix the powder with cool water, adding a little at a time until your goo is free of lumps and has reached the consistency of heavy cream. Let the mixture set while you are fiddling with the setup assembly; then check to see if either more water or more powder is needed.

Place one side back on the setup, clamping the bow end to the stem sheerline and the stern end to the transom, and making sure that the side lies so it is flat and snug against all the molds. If the side doesn't hit the sheer mark on the transom right on the nose, don't worry about it. Just adjust the transom up or down a bit. Make sure, however, that there is enough excess wood for the bottom bevel cut and enough left to shape the top of the tombstone. Of vital importance is that the side lies flat against the molds, and that the chine edges are not below the setup mold frames.

Satisfied? Then drive a nail through the side into the transom framing to hold it in place. Mark the sheer and the chine edges on the transom. Go to the bow and repeat the process. That done, pull the nail in the bow end and carefully let the panel spring clear of the stem. Check

your glue mixture and adjust it if necessary, then slather it along the stem. Clamp the forward end of the panel back to the stem, right on the line. Bore for your nails—staggering the holes about 2¹/₂" apart—drive them, and set the heads slightly with a 1/4" machinist's punch. Reach up under the jig as best you can to wipe up excess glue right on the spot.

Go to the stern and draw the nailing space limits that will keep your fastenings in the oak framing and out of the plywood of the transom face. To do this, eyeball the center of the framing, top and bottom, from the side, and use your straightedge to draw a line connecting the two points. Draw another line, aft of and parallel to the first; this represents the outer face of the plywood. Nail only between those lines, keeping the nails parallel to the face of the transom as you drive them into the framing. If this description isn't completely clear, you can tell what to do from the intent, which is to drive all nails into the oak framing. Don't cant them, or you may be faced with a porcupine effect inside the boat.

Now let the stern end of the panel swing free, slather on the glue, clamp it back in place, and proceed with the preboring and nailing procedure as for the bow.

Now I can employ the easiest of all

...h and 6' location marks are then laid ...ch chine.

The chine bevel is cut at 38 degrees on both sides so that the chine sheds water when installed. A small jig for holding the chine at the proper angle allows for quick and accurate smoothing with a belt sander.

An accurate fit at the chine ends is obtained by scribing the compound bevel on a short pattern, then transferring the cut to the actual chine.

instructions: Do the same thing on the other side.

A Money-saving Variation

Let's take a look at buttstrapping the sides, which would allow you to use two 4x8' plywood sheets instead of the single 4x16' one. Don't try scarf joints with 8' sheets, or the sides will come up short. Though the dory is 15'6" over-all, it is nearly 16' along the gunwale.

Using a 16' sheet is preferable, especially for appearance's sake. But, depending on where you live, it is possible that shipping costs alone for the long sheet would set you back an arm and a leg. So let's explore butt-strapping two short sheets. You won't lose anything in strength and general effectiveness.

After splitting the two 8' sheets lengthwise, butt the ends together, trace the side pattern on them, then buttstrap them right on the shop floor (using 3/8" plywood straps instead of the 1/2" shown on the plan), keeping the straps back from the edge by a distance equal to the width of the chines. Also remove the buttstrap thickness of 3/8" off mold No. 4, as it is obvious from the plan that there would be interference there on the forward edge.

I know this technique differs from that shown on the plan: "1/2x4' plywood buttstrap placed after hull is righted," and "fir frames port and starboard put in place after the hull is righted and butts strapped." These notes leave it to the builder to find some method of holding the ends of the plywood side panels together until this stage of construction is reached, and quite frankly I see no practical solution to this problem. If I decide to go in for building cheaper versions of this dory, one of my cost-saving moves would be buttstrapping, but I would fasten the straps on the floor, not on the jig, and not try to work out a temporary method suggested by the plans.

If you decide to buttstrap 8' sheets together, fasten the butts with flat-headed smooth-wire copper nails of the skinniest diameter. Driven without preboring, and with the points whacked over where they protrude, these will work just fine. If you lack copper nails, use screws, tacks, bolts—most anything except bronze Anchorfast-type nails, which will inevitably break off when you try to bend their points.

A Choice of Chines

Chines for the Gloucester Gull can be handled in one of three ways: (1) inside the chines, which are my choice; (2) outside chines, as shown in the lower left-hand corner of the plans; or (3) no chines at all, using the stitch method to hold the bottom to the sides. All three choices have advantages and disadvantages.

Placing the chine outside relieves you of all worries about fitting the ends, yet it is no easy chore to nail them from the inside, because of the hull's considerable side flare. Also, the changing bevel or twist to the sides raises a beveling problem for the chines when they are outside—the best you could do would be to cut a constant chine bevel of 28 degrees on your tablesaw, which would be about right for the bow area, and bevel the rest of the chine by planing after installation.

If outside chines are selected, the high edges of the sides should be beveled so they are flat across before the chines are put on. Otherwise the chines would have to be cut down by that much even if they were beveled first. All these complications seem hardly worth the trouble, especially since I don't like the look of outside chines on this hull.

If you have considerable expertise with working with glue and fiberglass cloth, you will have little trouble with the no-chine method. The sides and bottom are joined by wires and then the joint is glued with resin and fiberglass cloth. The wires are later removed and the joint beefed up with additional layers of fiberglass cloth, inside and out.

I think I will try this method myself if I should ever decide to build a cheaper and lighter model of this craft. In fact, because the bottom lies

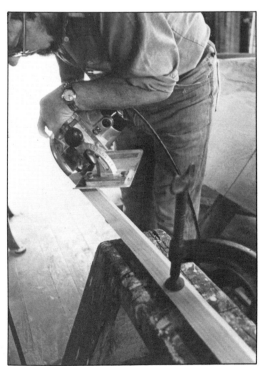

When the exact length has been determined for the chines, and the compound bevel marked on the ends, they can be cut with the circular saw set at 33 degrees.

Aligning the 6' reference marks exactly, you can clamp the chine in place at the center and check the fit at the ends. If it is slightly off, or long, it can be helped by running a sharp saw between the end and the stem or transom.

When all is well, spread the glue on chine, let it sit for a few minutes, a install it once more.

so fair on the sides and can be securely fastened to the stem and the transom, I doubt if there is any need to use wire at all. I would just fit the bottom carefully, round the edges of the joint 3/8" or so, and cover the whole bottom with glass cloth, bringing the edges over the sides for about 2½" overlap (I do this anyway on the standard model). I would do this right on the jig to hold the sides in place, then take the hull off after a day or so had passed. I would finish the job by reinforcing the joint from the inside, using either epoxy resin and filler or polyester resin and filler to build the joint out to a concave curve, and then lay on a couple of layers or more of glass cloth. The natural flare of the dory makes such an approach feasible—that is, if you like working with the gooey stuff. You save weight, and there's no oak chine to fit or rot.

To me, one disadvantage of the no-chine method is the time wasted while you wait for the glass to harden before you can continue with the rest of the building. I am just a bit impatient, and the idea of starting the hull assembly in the morning and throwing out the jig in the afternoon with the basic hull all done appeals to me. That's one of the reasons I stick with the inside chine method, which I'll now describe.

Chines are preferably cut from a 12' oak flitch (that's live-edged, with the bark on), if you can find one that long with a sweep in it that is as close as possible to the chine curve of your side pattern when it is laid flat on the floor. That's the true shape of the chine before it is installed, even though common sense and your eye indicate that the chines should match the rocker of the bottom profile.

I know that's hard to swallow, but believe me, it's true. You run into optical illlusions like this time and again when boatbuilding, and it is one reason why I have often been frustrated, but never bored, in pursuing this career. I still can count on learning something from every new boat I build for the first time, whether complex or a simple design.

So use the sweep of the tree to your advantage, and cut the chines as closely as you can to that curve. If you have only straight boards to work with that have some width to give you leeway, then strike a curve as close to optimum as you can get and saw to that. If you have narrow boards with no room for curves, you can still pull the chines in to fit; just plan on a harder job. If you run into any small knots or poor grain in your chine stock, keep them on the inside of the bend and you will have less breakage.

Chines sawn from straight-edged boards are very difficult to install if they are put in directly from the saw. The best procedure is to saw them out

well before they are needed and leave them outdoors to gather a little moisture. Don't try to put them in place the first time for good; rather, bend them around the outside of the hull along the chine line and leave them for a few hours or, preferably, overnight.

You can cut your chines from boards that are either 3/4" planed thickness on the flat, or from those that are 1⅛" thick, in which case you can take off slices with your portable circular saw set at 38 degrees. Either way, the chines should measure about 1⅜" on the flat and should be beveled the same on both edges. They should be double beveled like this so they will shed water when installed in the boat, and the bevel edge is no more difficult to fit than the square edge. Because the chine curve is about the same at both ends of the boat—unlike the gunwales which have reverse curve—the chines can be swapped end for end. Doing this means that you need to pay no attention to left and right.

If I had been leaning over Phil Bolger's shoulder when he drew that beveled chine, I would have urged him to draw the bevel from the high side, which would allow more wood for fastening. Likely his point of view favored a narrow piece of wood that would bend in more easily, but it's smaller than I want to drive a nail into blind, which is why I use a wider one even though it is less flexible.

it firmly in place, prebore and fasten into it Anchorfast nails. Check for excess glue and away with a damp cloth.

Cut off the excess length of stem and transom on the bottom, as well as the excess at the ends of the sides.

Plane down the remainder so that the joints are smooth and flush.

Plane the bottom edges of the sides flat and level with the chines so that the bottom will lie perfectly flat upon them.

To prevent any tendency of the sides to creep inward, due to the angle of the nails from the bottom, tack some small wedges between mold and chine wherever there are gaps.

On the bottom sheet is struck a centerlin which is then placed so it lines up precise with the centerlines of stem and transom

Bow and Stern Fit

For a pattern for fitting the ends of the chine, cut a foot-long piece of chine that is exactly the size you are using. Lay the pattern against the side just as the fitted chine will lie. Butt it up against the stem and scribe it for end fit. Set your table saw blade at 33 degrees and whack the pattern off to that mark. Use the other end for the transom fit; make that cut 38 degrees.

To get a perfect fit at both ends of the chine, transfer those cuts to the actual chine and determine the exact length of the chine, end to end.

Place your chine at a comfortable work height; sawhorses will do. (I use four, two for the work pieces and two for the dory as support when it's off the jig and ready for interior work.) Keeping in mind the chine curve, mark the bow end of your pattern on the chine stock. With the chine

clamped to a sawhorse, saw the end off to a 33-degree bevel. I use a portable circular saw for this cut.

Flip your chine over so you're looking at the side that fits against the skin of the hull. You're ready now to lay off the proper length, and locate the chine's exact placement when it goes into the boat. The best tool for this is a 6' wooden folding rule with an extension for inside measurement. Extend the rule to its full length, and

Prebore for 1 1/4" Anchorfast nails into the chines, following the angle of the sides.

Drive the nails from amidships out to the ends, but do not set the heads...

...until the slivers amidships are glued and t in place.

The curve of the sides is then traced on the sheet.

Remove and flip the bottom sheet, and cut the marked curve at a 30-degree bevel. If you're using a half-sheet, there will be a pair of short, straight-edged lengths amidships, along which slivers will be glued.

After spreading glue upon the chines, get some help and tack the bottom in place with a couple of finish nails.

lay it snugly right along the inside edge of the boat's side. Allow the rule to follow the curve of the side exactly as the chine will. Butt the end of the rule against the stem, making sure that the corner of the rule is snugly up against the stem. Put a mark on the side of the boat at the 6' mark.

Now, leaving your rule fully extended, place it on the beveled end of the inside chine corner, and mark 6' again. Get the idea? Those two 6'

marks establish the exact placement of the chine for installing—it's just a matter of matching the marks.

For the aft chine end measurement, butt your rule against the transom, fold up a couple of sections, and use the extension to meet the 6' mark. You have now established the total length of the chine as it lies against the skin of the boat, with only the after cut left to be made.

Pay careful attention when you

make that cut, because it's easy to make a mistake. Keep in mind that the last measurement to the transom represents the inside fit of the chine, so the bevel has to be added beyond that point or the chine will come up short.

Lay your pattern on the chine with its cut face touching the after total-length mark; project the cut face across the edge of the chine. Flip the chine over and use the pattern to draw the rake connecting those points.

Free the boat from the jig by cutting the stem and transom frame excess, and lifting her off.

There's nothing like a finished hull to give you a feeling of great accomplishment.

Saw at 38 degrees and you have it.

No matter how many times you do this, it is still easy to make mistakes. The most common ones are (1) forgetting to change your portable circular saw bevel from the 33-degree setting for the forward end to the 38 degrees before you make the after cut, and (2) cutting the stern bevel in the wrong direction. I've done both, and that's why I still stop and think before making any cuts.

Measuring and cutting the chines the way I have described it usually leaves a little room for scribing and final fit. If the end joint happens to be a bit slack, often you can adjust it by pulling the chine fore or aft, and up, one way or the other, and end up with a good fit. Put both of the chines in for a dry fit—first one and then the other, one at a time, so you will have room to slip a saw point along the stem or transom to cut them in place.

Because the chine ends are raked, they can't be dropped straight in on their aligning marks. Slip the bow end down the stem a bit, then, holding the chine into the side amidships by hand, swing the aft end of the chine inboard and tuck it down to the transom. Pull the chine aft until the marks on the chine and the side align.

You'll need about a dozen clamps to hold the chine tightly in place. Clamp it amidships first, then work toward both ends. Hook a clamp under the chine's edge, with the screw pad resting on the edge of the side, and any reluctant spot will be pulled exactly into place.

After the dry fit and the trimming, if any, apply glue liberally, put the chine back in place, and prebore and fasten it with 1" Anchorfast nails, driven from the outside. Stagger the nails about 3-4" apart. To avoid glue runoff, let the glue sit on the chine for a few minutes before installing it.

Closing In On Her

You're now about to make a complete boat of her, instead of a partly defined shape anchored to the molds.

The first step is to trim off the excess length of the stem and the transom. For now, too, trim the ends of the plywood sides straight across, flush with the stem, and do the same at the transom. Then plane the bottom of the chines down level, flat across. Check the fit with a straightedge long enough to sweep in an arc across the bottom's greatest width.

I recommend you plan carefully to get two bottom halves out of one 4 x 8' sheet of 1/2" plywood. Rip the sheet down the middle and buttstrap the two halves to get the length you'll need. This won't quite cover the entire bottom area, but it's a simple matter to achieve the needed width by adding just a sliver of plywood, 1/2" or less in width and something under 2' long, one at each side amidships, right by mold No. 4. There will be no loss in bottom strength, because the center seat frame is fastened to the bottom at this point, and because the bottom piece will go nearly to the outside edge of the chine at this point, where the widest gap is.

When you nail the bottom on, the sides will tend to creep in due to the excessive cant of the nails. To foil this distortion, cut some wooden wedges, and put one between the inboard side of the chine and the mold wherever little gaps show.

The bottom is fitted pie-crust fashion: lay the half sheet over the chines, tack it to the stem and the transom, and mark it all around the hull from underneath. Make sure it's centered, if you're using the half sheet, with equal gaps at each side amidships. Obviously, the way to do this is to mark a centerline on the panel and match it to the centerline at the bottom of the stem and the transom.

Remove the sheet and flip it over onto your sawhorses; clamp it down for sawing. With your saw set at 30 degrees, cut as close to your line as skill allows, remembering that the closer you come, the less you will have to trim off by hand. And the closer you come to the line, the easier it will be to see where you are nailing. You can be quite daring with this cut, because the sides will not swell out beyond your traced line—the pull of the nails will see to that.

Slather the chines with glue and

The mid-seat frame is fitted and marked off, so that holes can be bored from the inside for the nails.

The cant (side) frames are laid out on a piece of oak and cut out on the band saw.

With the cant frames glued and fastened to the sides, the mid-frame can be tied together with wood screws driven from forward.

tack the shaped bottom back on. Pre-bore for your 1¹/⁴" Anchorfast nails, spacing their locations 3¹/²" to 4" apart, making sure you are drilling through into the chine, and keeping the holes canted to match the flare of the side. Start driving the nails amidships and work out toward both ends.

Perhaps you're wondering, "Why not use screws?" There's not a thing wrong with them. I use nails because they are cheaper, faster, and available.

Free the stem, cut off the transom framing, and lift the hull off the jig. Now she can sit on the other set of saw horses. In your mind's eye you can see her in the water. No one will fault you for taking a little time off before you set about her interior finishing. Walk around her; sit back and gaze at her lines. You will no doubt agree with me that she has one of the most graceful hull shapes that can be built.

Finishing the Hull

To finish the hull, begin by striking a centerline down the inside of the bottom. From the plans, measure off the seat frame locations, and mark on which side of the indicators the seat frames will lie. The stern seat frame is 1-9-4 from the transom framing; the next is 3-11-0 forward, and the third is 4-0-0 forward of that. Square their locations to the centerline with dividers (the method you learned in school), or use a square where you can.

You'll find that having lost the support of the molds, the sides will have pulled in a little. When you measure across the gunwales amidships, at the greatest beam they will have lost a half-inch or so from the 3-11-2 gunwale-to-gunwale measurement inside the planking at the sheer.

To remedy this until further completion stiffens the hull, cut a stick 47¹/⁴" long, bevel the ends to match the sides, and cram the top edge down flush to the gunwales, about an inch forward of where the cant frame will go so the stick will not interfere with the frame's placement, and drive a nail through the outside of the hull into each end. Leave this stretcher in place until all the framing is in, and take it out only when the gunwales are ready to be installed.

The seat frames are all 5¹/²" wide, and all land on the mold stations. Using your scale, measure them off the plans, allowing a little extra length for a scribed fit. If you prefer, you can get their general shape off the jig, since they fall on stations. It doesn't matter whether the frames are exactly plumb to the base line or not—what is important is that they are properly located.

The mid-seat frame goes in square, no bevel anywhere. Fit it to the sides and bottom, and mark all around. Take it out and bore out through the hull from inside for 1¹/⁴" nails. Glue it

lavishly, put it back in place, bore back through the same holes, and fasten it for good.

Now put the two cant frames in, fastening them with the same procedure and the same size nails, plus three 1¹/⁴" No. 10 bronze wood screws fastened from forward so they won't show.

The stern seat-frame end cut is beveled 12 degrees, the top bevel is 5 degrees, and the bottom is 4 degrees. The seat riser tops are beveled 38 degrees, and the end cuts butted to the frame take a 13-degree setting for both the table saw and the miter gauge. Keep right and left in mind for these cuts. The center seat risers are 7³/⁸" long, with a top bevel of 36 degrees.

For the bow seat frame, the end cut takes 15 degrees, with 5 degrees for the top and 4 degrees for the bottom. Use 30 degrees for the seat riser tops, and for the end cuts use 13 degrees— the same for the stern risers.

All these risers can be made from leftover chine scrap, should you have been so unfortunate as to saw some out with poor grain, knots, etc. Just resaw the bevels for the mid- and bow-seats; the bevel is OK as-is for the stern seat. Fasten all the risers and foot stretchers with 1" nails. (If you are six feet tall or over, you will have to locate the foot stretchers farther aft than indicated on the plans.)

The breasthook is OK as shown on the plans, and fully effective, at least

of the way the angles converge,
seat-frame and risers require care
layout and bevel.

As with the risers, the foot stretchers can be made out of leftover chine stock.

The slightly modified breasthook is cut to shape on the band saw.....

functionally. However, I prefer to make it slightly ornamental, and to my mind more shipshape, by curving its aft surface with a concave cutout and fitting it right against the stem instead of leaving an opening there. The side cut requires a 25-degree bevel, and the stem fit 43 degrees. Fasten on each side with two 1" nails and mark the locations of the nails so the gunwale fastenings won't run into them.

Preferably, the gunwales should be cut from live-edge 16' oak, either board or plank. Again, just as with the chines, the best stock will have a sweep or curve to the grain that approximates as closely as possible the shape of the side pattern. Cut a 30-degree bevel on the bottoms of the gunwales; this will allow the $1\frac{1}{2}$" oak to bend on much more easily. Once again, take notice that, unlike the chines, the gunwales cannot be swapped end for end—their reverse curve prohibits that.

Installing the gunwales calls for quite a few clamps—16 is none too many. Glue the gunwales lavishly, and starting at the bow, clamp them about every foot or so. A helper comes in most handy here, but if you don't have one, prop up the after end of the gunwale on a horse or something high enough so you can start clamping at the bow end and keep the gunwale parallel with the sheer. You can work it along from there alone.

Fasten the gunwales from the inside, preboring for nails 5" or 6" apart and staggered somewhat. At the stem bore two 3/8" holes for oak bungs on each side—one in the stem, one in the breasthook—and follow these borings again, this time for $1\frac{1}{2}$" nails.

After nailing the first gunwale, saw the bow end flush with the stem, so it won't interfere with the other gunwale. Dip the bungs in glue and tap them into place over the nail-heads, being mindful of matching their grain with that of the gunwale.

When you reach the stern, you'll find that it's virtually impossible to get a nail into the transom framing and not run into it later when you're rounding the gunwale ends off, so don't bother. Instead, drive two 1" nails as close to the framing as possible, from the inside, when you are doing the rest of the fastening. Except for those two nails, there's no need to set the heads of the gunwale fastenings; just whack them in with determination. At the transom, let the gunwale ends project 1/16", so that wood and fiberglass can all be smoothed down together later when you sheathe the transom.

Now is the time to put in the foundations for the oarlocks. Note that the plans show the oarlocks sitting plumb, with the boring for the shanks going right through the gunwale. Phil Bolger, the designer, believes this arrangement is better than mounting them in line with the flare of the sides.

I keep them in an upright position by making four cleats, $6\frac{3}{4}$" x 3/4 x $1\frac{1}{2}$", beveled to conform to the side flare. The after cleats are glued and screwed, centered $10\frac{1}{2}$" from the after side of the cant frames, and the forward ones are centered 4'1" from their centers. The oarlock side plates and the horns are Wilcox Crittenden, No. 4482 and No. 4477 respectively. They're not quite as neat as the designer's, I think, but they are rugged and much easier to install.

With the dory still upright, draw the shape of the top of the tombstone on both faces of the transom. Bore a $2\frac{1}{4}$" hole for the scull notch, well up; some builders have made this too low and have reported that water slops in when the boat is in a steep chop. To get rid of excess wood fast, make a couple of diagonal saw cuts from the top down to the gunwale, holding the saw about parallel to the sheer. I use a Skil saw for as much as I can, but right here I don't recommend it unless your nerves are all set to have the sawed piece drop down on the blade and go flying. To avoid this, use the Skil saw to cut part way through, and finish the job with a handsaw.

Take down the remainder of the wood with a chisel, block plane, spoke shave, and wood rasps, all of which can contribute to fairing the transom down to the gunwales with ease and near perfection. Round off the inside edge of the notch, but leave the out-

...then fitted tightly against the stem. Mark where the fastenings are, so as to avoid them when fastening the gunwales.

Glue and clamp the gunwales in place, and fasten them from the inside.

At the stern, drive two nails from the inside, as close to the transom frame as possible.

side edge square until you glass the transom.

Use a sharp block plane to smooth the top of the gunwales almost flush with the side, then finish smooth with a belt sander, using 60-grit paper. Cut the bungs off about 1/8" high first, to allow for poor grain, then cut them flush.

Now you can fix the seat tops in place. Make them from 1/2" plywood, either marine or exterior grade, and fasten them with 1 1/4" No. 10 bronze or brass screws. Counterbore for these; a Fuller countersink, which comes in screw sizes from No. 6 to No. 14, is very handy here.

If, when you're boring, you think you have hit one of the fastenings in the seat riser, try driving a screw there. If the driven screw meets one of your nail fasteners, and you keep on driving, it will back the nail right out through the side of the boat. I've had this ruin a highly finished paint job. It's almost incredible that the turning action of a screw can drive out an Anchorfast nail, in oak, at a 90-degree angle to the axis of the driven screw. Believe me, it can.

With the interior woodwork complete, it's time to put some armor coating on her bottom.

Bottom Insurance Policy

Your dory is upside down on sawhorses now, ready for "preparing the surface," as they say in all the instructions having to do with prettying or protecting the surface of any wooden structure.

Trim the edges of the bottom exactly to the flare of the sides. A small hand-held power plane will make short work of this. Round the bottom's edges 3/8"; do the same to the stem and the transom edges.

For your sanding work, tack a sanding belt or a good length of sanding paper to a board that is about a foot or more long. Using an ordinary short sanding block invites creating a scalloped effect caused by the hard and soft spots typical of plywood surfaces.

Fill all nail holes and any other uglies with auto body filler or any non-oil-based putty, mixing no more than a golf ball-size lump at a time, because the stuff sets up fast; mixing any more than that means losing much of it. If the mix is stiffer than you like, add a little polyester resin to thin it down.

A variation on auto body filler is a material called "spot putty," which is available in auto supply stores. It comes in a toothpaste tube and needs no mixing. It doesn't work well in deep dents, but is great for hairline cracks and hammer dimples, and is easy to sand.

Clean your putty knife with acetone or lacquer thinner just the second you are done with a batch, or expect to face a rock-hard mass that will have to be dealt with before you use it again.

Sand all the filled holes lightly, and sand away slivers or any other irregularity that will catch and snag your fiberglass cloth. Sweep the dust from all areas to be glassed, and sweep your shop floor clear, too, because this is one job where it pays to be squeaky clean; picking shavings out of a dropped piece of glass cloth is a time-waster if there ever was one.

Here's what you'll need for the job:
4 yards of 38" 10-ounce cloth
1 gallon of polyester resin,
    with hardener
1 3" roller
1 2½" or 3" paint brush
1 pint of acetone, minimum
2 or 3 quart milk containers,
    top half cut off

A half-gallon of resin will do the job, if you make no mistakes—a full gallon allows for plenty of them. There are two kinds of polyester resin commonly available. One is air-inhibiting; this contains wax, which helps the drying process somewhat. The other is called "lay-up," and needs no sanding between coats; it is usually available at any sizeable boatyard, where it is often cheaper than the same product at a marine supply store.

I use the lay-up type for reasons of economy, and because it allows me to leave the job unfinished if I have to (one of those long, long phone calls). The surface will provide a good bond without any sanding when I get back

The cleats for the oarlock sockets are beveled to let the oarlocks stand plumb. Glue and fasten them in place.

After drawing out the shape of the top of the transom, bore a 2¼" hole for the sculling notch, but not too low.

A quick way to rough out the shape of the transom top is with the Skil saw—but only if you're careful.

x

When you take a hard look at the rising material costs, it makes sense to consider the possibility of accepting some compromises and making some concessions at the expense of quality when you plan to build any boat. Let's examine the Bolger Type VI dory from this point of view.

Back in 1967, a 4 x 16' sheet of 3/8" marine grade plywood sold for about $30, and a 4 x 12' sheet of 1/2" for about $20. These prices have since tripled, and there's no reason to believe they won't continue to rise. In addition, marine plywood in lengths greater than 8' is increasingly difficult to find.

So far, the only concession I've made in building these dories has been the use of half-sheets to get two bottoms out of one sheet of plywood, which calls for a little piecing out. This is a rather minor savings—about $35 per boat, at current prices—but definitely worth the trouble.

I am suggesting that more drastic changes might well be acceptable if they mean the difference between building and not building the dory at all.

You could forget marine grade plywood, and reduce the thickness, and still have a sufficiently strong hull. Then you need buy only three 4 x 8' sheets of 1/4" AC exterior grade. This means butting your side and bottom panels with 1/4" ply butts with their grain going fore and aft, and letting the bottom butt joint fall just ahead of the mid-seat. You could buy one 16' 2x4 from which to cut chines and gunwales, and settle for another 16' board of pine, spruce, or whatever for seat risers and transom frames; you could fabricate the stem from a couple of pieces of 2x6 glued together. A dory built this way, glass and all, weighs slightly less than 85 lbs.

At the time of writing, this package would cost about $40, as compared with $200 for the corresponding bill of basic hull materials specified for use in the preceding instructions. Beyond that you could forget varnish and use paint throughout, and you could substitute galvanized oarlocks for brass. You could also buy galvanized instead of brass or bronze fastenings.

You gain two things by this approach: a reduction in cost and a reduction in weight. You lose your yacht finish, you expend a little more time, and you lose some degree of strength and life expectancy for the craft.

If you were to build more than one dory, it would pay to buy a sheet, or sheets, of 1/4" x 12' marine plywood fo

to it the next day. If you decide to use the air-inhibiting type, be sure you will be able to finish the whole job without any lengthy breaks. Otherwise, sanding will show up scabby places where the coats haven't completely bonded. Arrange for about three uninterrupted hours for the job.

Temperature and humidity are very critical factors in the curing of polyester resin. High humidity slows down the curing time, as do cold temperatures. A dry day with a temperature of about 70 is ideal.

Start by laying your cloth over the bottom of the boat, with one edge overlapping the side about 2½". With your shop brush, smooth out all wrinkles, then trim the edges piecrust style, leaving a 2½" overlap all around, including the stem and transom, and set these aside. There's nothing really fussy about it: for the transom, take a piece from either end of the excess cloth, which is already wide enough— just cut it long enough to cover the transom and overlap the bottom. Don't bother cutting out a hole for the

scull notch; save that for next day. The stem will take a piece of cloth about 6" wide and long enough to overlap the bottom.

Pour out about a pint of resin into one of the cut-down milk containers— that's what I use; perhaps you would prefer something else. A pint is plenty if you are blessed with warm hands. Add one teaspoon of hardener if the day is a bit cool with some moisture in the air, and a bit less if the day is warm and dry. The makeup of the mixture doesn't have to be precise for a good

After roughing it out, the shape can be worked with a chisel, a plane, a spokeshave, and wood rasps.

With the gunwales faired smooth, the seats can now be fitted and fastened in place.

The interior woodwork is complete, so the dory is turned upside down so that corners and edges can be smoothed and rounded.

the bottoms. Such a sheet sells for a little more than $30. Since you can get two one-piece bottoms from a sheet, it eliminates the buttstrap. A bottom for a boat will cost about $15. Doing it the other way using one sheet of ¼" x 8' AC or BC ply costs about $10 per sheet, which will produce a saving if you are going to build only one boat but no savings if you are going to build a fleet.

I would use a spruce skeg in place of the oak one shown on the plans and have changed those 2" x 14 screws to 2" stainless panhead in whatever wire size is available. It seems to me that the 2" x 14 flat-headed screws are overkill by the time their heads are buried in the ¼" bottom. I would use three sizes of panheads to fasten the skeg; 1" for the first fastening at the pointy end toward the bow, 1½" for the next one aft, then three of the 2" for the rest.

If you still prefer the heavier dory with 3/8" sides and ½" bottom, don't try to economize with 3/8" 3-ply exterior. Because of its thin outer layers and thick water-absorbing core, 3/8" ply is not worth lugging home.

There is, however, a 3/8" 4-ply exterior that shows some promise of holding together. Even though two layers run in the same direction, it has held up well on the bottom of a skiff of mine used now for three seasons. Whether it is commonly available I don't know, but I found mine at a local lumber supplier. I'd use two sheets of the 3/8" 4-ply for the sides, and one sheet of 1/2" exterior for the bottom, if I wanted the heavier dory.

More likely than not, considering the stress of economic conditions today, the economy model dory, like the economy car, comes out the winner. Most of us have fewer dollars to spend, in terms of real purchasing power, and the cost of building a boat represents a greater sacrifice in terms of what other expenditures must be given up to accommodate it.

I like to go first class when it comes to building any boat. I suggest these concessions only because they become a necessity. More often than before, I find myself wondering if the economy model shouldn't be an option I offer my customers. And I face the possibility that it may well have to supercede entirely the standard model as I still build it.

I do not recommend this reduction in standards, but I submit it for serious consideration by any would-be builder who cannot afford the luxury of first class in these inflationary times.

---

job. What is important is that the boat is not in direct sunlight, and that the mix is stirred thoroughly, with special attention to the corners if you are using a square container. You can tell when the batch is mixed enough, because it will turn slightly darker than the uncatalyzed resin.

Put on a face mask that filters out fumes, and go to it. Pour out a glob of resin amidships and use your 3" roller to work the resin out from the center toward the edges in all directions. Continue to work in an ever-widening pattern. That first pint will very nearly do the whole bottom. When it's used up, mix another pint immediately. This will be enough to finish the bottom, and the stem and transom pieces.

You'll find it's a bit tricky to pour the resin along the side overlap and catch it with your roller before it runs down the side of your boat. Here you might want to use a brush.

After the bottom is thoroughly stuck down all around, and you see the wood grain everywhere as though you were looking through a coat of varnish, cover the bare wood of the stem and the transom with resin and lay the pieces of cloth into this fresh wet coat. This will keep the pieces in place. At the stem, overlap the cloth onto the bottom, trim the corners somewhat rounded, put more resin on, and work the cloth along the stem onto the bottom without cutting it. Cover the transom the same way. Don't waste time with wrinkles that won't budge with brush or roller pressure—grab hold of the cloth and give it a pull.

...ng non-oil-based putty, fill all irregulari-... in the surface, going over it more than ...e, if necessary, and sand the surfaces ...ooth.

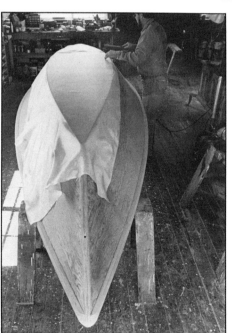
When temperature and humidity conditions are right, begin the sheathing with the bottom. Smooth out all wrinkles with a brush.

With the cloth smoothed out, begin to saturate it thoroughly, working out from the center in all directions.

Then roll or brush the cloth down smooth again.

By the time you get all your cloth down and impregnated with resin, the bottom will be thirsty again, especially the edge grain, so don't stop. Mix up another pint of resin and go over the entire area again. This should be enough. There will be a little resin left over, so go back over the job looking for starved spots, which will show up as grey areas and pinholes, and use up your resin on those.

You will have spent about two hours nonstop to reach this point. You will have used three pints of resin, and the cloth should be well saturated, which will ensure that it sticks and stays stuck. Plop your brush or roller in acetone and take a break before you put on the final coat—a short break if you're using air-inhibiting resin, and as long as you want if you're using the lay-up type.

Either way, keep your eye on the surface, and when the resin loses its glossy look—usually in from 15 minutes to half an hour—it is time to pour on the final coat. The final coat entirely hides the weave of the cloth, adds a protective gloss, and completes a smooth and glossy finish. For the best results, flow this one on with a brush to make a thicker coat.

Shake your brush free of acetone, and mix up the final pint of resin. I cut down the half-gallon container for this, because the brush fits better. Carefully brush in one direction, to build an even coat, *so you won't have*

to go back over it. This is vital, for if you do go back over it, say 10 or 15 minutes later, to hit a bare spot, that swipe you take isn't going to dry for days, and possibly never.

I had glassed a good many boats before I learned to avoid that touch-up swipe. At first I put the blame on insufficiently mixed resin, but eventually, knowing that I was using enough hardener and that I had stirred the mix thoroughly, I decided the cause to be the mysterious properties of the hardening process, the chemistry of which I know nothing.

What is readily apparent is that the larger the mass, the quicker it hardens. So when you take a thin swipe at a bare spot, don't be surprised if it stays tacky.

Wash your brush and roller in two rinses of acetone and put them away. If you plan on doing more fiberglassing, save the acetone. Put it in a can of its own, and when next you do glass work, plop your brush and roller in it first and use fresh acetone for rinsing. Following that procedure, I've used the same paint brush on more than 100 bottoms so far, and it looks as though it will be good for 100 more. I can't say as much for the rollers.

Once the job is dry, the sooner you start sanding, the easier it will be. In warm weather only a few hours of setting up time, sometimes even less, is sufficient. Plan to wait two hours.

When sanding, wear a dust mask and protective clothing whether you are going to work indoors or out.

The bottom of the boat always dries first, so start there. Quite likely there will be tacky spots on the feather edges of the overlap. Ignore them for now. As long as you do the bottom first and thus avoid filling your sandpaper with resin, these spots will give way to the sander when you get to them.

I use two sanders—a 3 x 21 belt sander and a heavy-duty Rockwell vibrator that takes a half sheet of paper—and use 60-grit paper with both. I begin with the belt sander to quickly cut down the surface and make it flat. It leaves scratches, but the vibrator erases those with ease. The belt sander is tricky to use; you must avoid tipping it, and you must always keep it moving in a sweeping motion. When you are sanding the side overlap, hold the sander flat to the surface. Don't ever hit a corner with it, or you will break through the glass and be onto bare wood in one quick, unfortunate pass. Sand the chine corners lightly with the vibrator later, and finish them by hand; likewise with the stem and transom edges.

To keep cloth corners from showing through the paint, feather them out by sanding or fill them out with auto body putty. The choice is a tossup, as far as I'm concerned—sand or fill out, whichever you prefer.

When you're finished, shake the dust out of the sanders, wipe them clean, and head for the showers. The latter will occur to you without my suggestions, I assure you.

The oak skeg, which you have

The resin is easiest applied with a 3" roller except along the boat's sides where a brush works better. It takes about a quart (mixed in two one-pint batches) to do the bottom and the stem and transom pieces.

The stem and transom require an undercoat of resin on the wood so that the cloth will adhere somewhat until it is saturated in place.

The final coat fills the weave of cloth and provides a protective finish.

scribed to fit the bottom, goes on next. Mark a centerline from stem to stern, and center the skeg on it. Trace around the skeg and mark the locations of the fastenings, being careful to keep them clear of the aft seat frame.

Bore pilot holes down through the hull for three 2" #10 bronze wood screws. Apply bedding compound to the underside of the skeg and put it back in place. You must fasten it from the inside, which means you will need someone or something to hold it in place. A helper is best, but if you don't have one, a weighted piece of 3 x 3 clamped to the skeg will do the trick.

Prebore for the screws from underneath, beginning with the forward screw. Don't countersink for the head — leave the wood there for pulling strength when you take up on it, and bury the screw head flush. Soap the screw first to ease the driving, and use a screwdriver bit in a bit brace for the job. You need two sizes of bits.

Check to see that the skeg is still in place and proceed with the rest of the screws. Clean off the squished-out bedding compound and you're done, since the skeg is not fiberglassed.

Painting a Lady

I have always thought that a first-class building job deserves a first-class paint job. Many builders appear to settle for second-rate, or worse, when it comes to painting a boat, no matter how much care they may have put into building her. I think it is because they don't feel capable of doing any better.

If you exercise proper care, and pay full attention to each of the several steps required to produce a superior finish, I can guarantee that you will give your boat an effective protective skin and a deep, glossy mirror surface that will delight your eye.

At least it's worth a try.

The first coat should be a thin, clear wood sealer, such as International #1026 or clear Firzite. You may prefer Firzite Interior White, which serves as a sealant and at the same time adds a foundation of pigment. All three go on fast, don't raise the grain, and leave a smooth, receptive surface for successive coats.

Some builders use epoxy, some a polyester resin, and there are those who choose an anti-rot preservative, such as Cuprinol. I don't know which of these is most effective in preventing crazing — that is, hairline cracks in plywood caused by the sun — so you're on your own.

Two quarts of regular wood sealer will be adequate for your entire boat, including the oars. On top of that, one coat of undercoat and one coat of finish paint is satisfactory, but for my money you need two coats of each, including the undercoats, for a yachty finish.

Today there are many kinds of paint on the market that do a good job, but require the use of their own special thinners, dryers, extenders, etc. If you happen to run out of any of these magic ingredients in the middle of a paint job, you are plain out of luck.

I still cling to the old-fashioned oil-based paints that I can doctor myself. On a hot, dry day when the paint drags and overlaps pile up, a slug of linseed oil takes care of the matter in a hurry. If the weather is cool and damp, a dash of Japan drier (unfortunately now difficult to get) sets the paint up nicely for sanding without a long wait between coats.

If the thought of chipped paint revealing layers of a different color upsets you, use a neutral base undercoater to which you have added one part in four of the pigment of your finish paint. I also recommend adding a third finish coat for a virtually impenetrable protective finish, under conditions of normal use. Also, when all your coats are uniform in pigment, you can wash your brushes out in plain gasoline between coats and keep right on going.

Varnish the seats with three coats, and leave the screw heads unfilled so you can remove them. The oak rails, stem head, and breasthook should be given a coat of Interlux 1643 natural wood filler first, followed by three or more coats of varnish, for a deeper finish.

Splice a 3/8" or 1/2" painter into a tight fitting hole bored about 15" below the stemhead, and the dory is finished. You have a boat you can be proud of, a boat that has turned the heads of observers the world over.

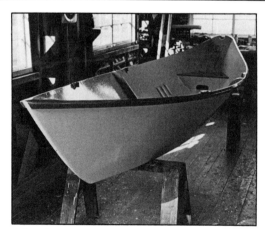

A first class building job deserves a first class finish job.

hen the sheathing has been sanded, the
eg is fitted to the bottom, directly on the
nter line.

Aligned with index marks, it can be
clamped and weighted in place to allow it
to be fastened from the inside.

Plans for the Gloucester Type VI Light Dory
are available from Harold H. Payson & Co.,
Pleasant Beach Road, South Thomaston,
Maine 04858. Drawn to a scale of $1\frac{1}{2}''$ to the
foot, they include a construction plan and a
scaled side pattern. They are $25 for the set.

Suggested Reading

Atkinson, Bob. "As Old as the Dory," *WoodenBoat* No. 18, Sept./Oct. 1984.

Bingham, Fred P. *Practical Yacht Joinery*. Camden, ME: International Marine Publishing Co., 1983.

Birmingham, Richard. *Boat Building Techniques Illustrated*. Camden, ME: International Marine Publishing Co., 1984.

Bolger, Philip C. *Bolger Boats*. Camden, ME: International Marine Publishing Co., 1983.

Bray, Maynard. *Mystic Seaport Museum Watercraft*. Mystic, CT: Mystic Seaport Museum, 1979.

Bureau of Ships, U.S. Navy. *Wood: A Manual for Its Use as a Shipbuilding Material*. Kingston, MA: Teaparty Books, 1983.

Carter, Lee & Evers. "Swampscott Dories," *WoodenBoat* No. 36, Sept./Oct. 1980.

Chapelle, Howard I. *Boatbuilding*. New York: W.W. Norton & Co., 1969.

Day, Jane. "Lowell's Boat Shop," *WoodenBoat* No. 27, Mar./Apr. 1979.

Fine Woodworking Editors. *Fine Woodworking on Joinery*. Newton, CT: The Taunton Press, 1979.

Gardner, John. *Building Classic Small Craft: Volume I*. Camden, ME: International Marine Publishing Co., 1977.

——— *Building Classic Small Craft: Volume II*. Camden, ME: International Marine Publishing Co., 1984.

——— *The Dory Book*. Camden, ME: International Marine Publishing Co., 1978.

McIntosh, David C. *How to Build a Wooden Boat*. Brooklin, ME. WoodenBoat Publications, Inc., 1987.

Payson, Harold H. *Build the Instant Catboat*. Camden, ME: International Marine Publishing Co., 1986.

——— *Build the New Instant Boats*. Camden, ME: International Marine Publishing Co., 1984.

——— *Instant Boats*. South Thomaston, ME: Harold H. Payson, 1985.

——— *Keeping the Cutting Edge*. Brooklin, ME: WoodenBoat Publications, Inc. 1983.

Rabl, S.S. *Boatbuilding in Your Own Backyard*. Centreville, MD: Cornell Maritime Press, 1958.

Sainsbury, John. *Planecraft: A Woodworker's Handbook*. New York· Sterling Publishing Co., 1984.

Simmons, Walter J. *Finishing*. Lincolnville Beach, ME: Walter J. Simmons, 1984.

——— *Lapstrake Boatbuilding*. Lincolnville Beach, ME: Walter J. Simmons, 1983.

Smith, Hervey Garrett. *Boat Carpentry*. New York: Van Nostrand Reinhold Co., 1965.

Steward, Robert M. *Boatbuilding Manual*. Camden, ME: International Marine Publishing Co., 1980.

Taube, Allen. *The Boatwright's Companion*. Camden, ME: International Marine Publishing Co., 1986.

Taylor, Roger C. *The Elements of Seamanship*. Camden, ME: International Marine Publishing Co., 1982.

Turner, Rich. "Colorado Dories," *WoodenBoat* No. 15, Mar./Apr. 1976.

Vaitses, Allan H. *Lofting*. Camden, ME: International Marine Publishing Co., 1980.

Watson, Alden A. *Hand Tools: Their Ways and Workings*. New York: W.W. Norton & Co., 1982.

White, Mark. "Ed Opheim's Dories," *WoodenBoat* No. 43, Nov./Dec. 1981.

Witt, Glen L. and Ken Hankinson. *Boatbuilding with Plywood*. Bellflower, CA: Glen-L Marine, 1978.

——— *How to Build Boat Trailers*. Bellflower, CA: Glen-L Marine, 1967.

WoodenBoat Magazine. *Boatbuilding Woods: A Directory of Suppliers*. Brooklin, ME: WoodenBoat Publications, Inc., 1987.

——— *The Directory of Wooden Boat Builders*. Brooklin, ME: WoodenBoat Publications, Inc., 1986.

——— *How to Build the Catspaw Dinghy*. Brooklin, ME: WoodenBoat Publications, Inc., 1986.

——— *WoodenBoat: An Appreciation of the Craft*. Reading, MA: Addison-Wesley Publishing Co., 1982.

Zimmermann, Jan. "Building the Banks Dory," *WoodenBoat* No. 19, Nov./Dec. 1977.

Books and *WoodenBoat* issues are all available from WoodenBoat Publications, P.O. Box 78, Brooklin, Maine 04616, 1-800-225-5205 or (in Maine) 207-359-4652. Call or write for a copy of our free merchandise catalog.

Plans Catalog

Fifty Wooden Boats: A Catalog of Building Plans

This comprehensive catalog presents 50 designs for a wide variety of boats—power, sail, and rowing—from prams and skiffs to bassboats, from rowing shells and catboats to schooners, from 7-footers to 40-footers. These designs are from some of the most distinguished naval architects of this century, including John Alden, Eldredge-McInnis, B.B. Crowninshield, Fenwick Williams, George Stadel, and Thomas Gillmer. Each design is fully described, with study plans and tables that summarize "vital statistics" (including cost estimates, skill required, and more). There is a chapter on "How to Understand Boat Plans" by Weston Farmer, a perspective drawing identifying the parts of a boat, and a bibliography of useful books and articles on boatbuilding. Finally, there are pages briefly describing the classic half-model plans offered by WoodenBoat. $11.95 from WoodenBoat.